WHEN THE WILL OF GOD IS A BITTER CUP

healing for the brokenhearted

WHEN THE WILL OF GOD IS A BITTER CUP

healing for the brokenhearted

Dr. Don Woodard

AMBASSADOR INTERNATIONAL
GREENVILLE, SOUTH CAROLINA & BELFAST, NORTHERN IRELAND

www.ambassador-international.com

WHEN THE WILL OF GOD IS A BITTER CUP
healing for the brokenhearted

ISBN: 978-1-935507-07-9

Cover Design & Page Layout by David Siglin of A&E Media

All Scripture quotations are from The King James Bible

AMBASSADOR INTERNATIONAL
Emerald House
427 Wade Hampton Blvd.
Greenville, SC 29609, USA
www.ambassador-international.com

AMBASSADOR PUBLICATIONS
Providence House
Ardenlee Street
Belfast, BT6 8QJ, Northern Ireland, UK
www.ambassador-productions.com

The colophon is a trademark of Ambassador

In Memory Of
Alysia Ruth Haak

Born
September 30, 1992
In Heaven
December 28, 2002

Accepted her bitter cup with courage.
Now walking on that Golden Street with Angels
and jumping on Heaven's trampoline.

For S.J.P.

"…beauty for ashes,

the oil of joy for mourning,

the garment of praise for the spirit of heaviness;

that they might be called trees of righteousness,

the planting of the Lord,

that He might be glorified."

Isaiah 61:3

TABLE OF CONTENTS

Foreword by Dr. Tom Wallace	11
Introduction	13
He Heals the Broken in Heart	15
Entering Into Gethsemane	19
Is It Possible For The Will Of God To Be A Bitter Cup?	25
It's OK If You Don't Like The Bitter Cup	29
A Little Farther	35
That I May Know Him	37
Surrender	39
God Cares That You Hold A Bitter Cup	43
Don't Be Critical Of Those Who Are Unable To Drink From Your Cup	47
Don't Retaliate Against Those Who Do Not Understand	51
God Is In Control	53
Trust God	55
The Right Way To Give Up	57
The Ultimate Purpose of The Will Of God	59
God Is Always On Time	61
God Can Get To Where You Are	65
A Time To Weep	69
Resurrection Morning Is Coming	75
These Words Are True And Faithful	79
What About The Palsied Man?	81
Heaven	85
Scripture Readings for Encouragement	87
About the Author	100

FOREWORD

Dr. Don Woodard has given us an excellent book of encouragement and enlightenment on how to cope and handle the many difficult seasons of life. For those of us who have been to the funeral home and to the grave, there is truth that we relate to. Those presently going through the valley will find a friend in this volume. All who read will do well to become more familiar with the principles given, because everybody's time of need will come sooner or later.

Dr. Woodard has shown us from the accounts of Joseph, Job, David, Mary and Martha, and Jesus Himself that there is purpose in what the Heavenly Father allows to come into the lives of His children. He has given us an abundance of scriptures from which to draw strength. It is far better to learn from the materials we read, or from the experiences of others, than to learn from our own personal experiences.

Pastors and counselors should welcome this comforting manual to pass along to those who are hurting. The reader will find the material to be practical, down to earth, and right where people live, and will realize that the message they are hearing comes from one who has been there, done that, and got the "T" shirt.

—Dr. Tom Wallace

INTRODUCTION

This book began as a sermon I preached for several months around the country and it seemed that everywhere the Lord led me to preach it people were encouraged. I then felt led to put it in a booklet and the Lord also seemed to use that. After more study thought and counseling with people who have experienced a bitter cup in their lives I decided to rewrite a few chapters and add several more. So what you have in your hands is the result of lessons learned from others who have had challenges, suffered losses and drank from a bitter cup.

It has been my joy and privilege to travel the country serving my Saviour as an evangelist since 1993. In my travels I have met people who have experienced trying times, storms, and hardships. Many are good Godly dedicated Christian people whom God had allowed to receive a bitter cup in various times of life.

When hardships come our way we must take positive Biblical action. Such trials can either make us bitter or make us better. Tragedies can either completely defeat us or they can teach us to be a blessing to others.

The end result of our trials, tribulations, heartaches and the bitter cups we receive in life is often up to us. We do not always have the power to choose our circumstances, but we do have the power to choose what we do with our circumstances and we have the power to choose what our circumstances do with us.

My prayer is that this book will be a blessing to you—as its principles have been a blessing to me in those hours that I held a bitter cup in my hands.

Until I see HIM,
Dr. Don Woodard

chapter 1

HE HEALS THE BROKEN IN HEART

PSALMS 147:3

3) He healeth the broken in heart, and bindeth up their wounds.

LUKE 4:16-19

16) And he came to Nazareth, where he had been brought up: and, as his custom was, he went into the synagogue on the Sabbath day, and stood up for to read.

17) And there was delivered unto him the book of the prophet Esaias. And when he had opened the book, he found the place where it was written,

18) The Spirit of the LORD is upon me, for he hath anointed me to preach the   gospel to the poor; he hath sent me to heal the brokenhearted, to preach deliverance to the captives, and recovering of sight to the blind, to set at liberty them that are bruised,

19) To preach the acceptable year of the LORD.

There is a healer of the broken hearted, there is one who understands our bitter cup and has experienced every kind of heart ache we can imagine or will ever experience. His name is Jesus Christ and He is the healer of the broken hearted.

After Jesus had returned from the wilderness where he had been fasting for forty days and was tempted of the Devil for forty days, in Luke Chapter four we find Him in the synagogue in His hometown of Nazareth. These were the people who knew Him as the carpenter's son, not as the only begotten Son of God, perhaps many of these folks at the synagogue had watched him grow up. Here setting among them in the synagogue at the beginning of His earthly ministry He proclaims who He is and what His purpose for being on earth is. In His proclamation He includes that He was sent "to heal the broken hearted". Oh friend, what comfort, what hope in knowing that this one who is the Son of God was sent for many a great purpose and one of them is that He came to heal the broken hearted, He is the healer of the broken hearted.

Consider His qualifications as healer of the broken hearted. He is the creator, the only begotten Son of God and He is God clothed in humanity. Other qualifications are found in Hebrews 4:14-16.

14) Seeing then that we have a great high priest, that is passed into the heavens, Jesus the Son of God; let us hold fast our profession.
15) For we have not an high priest which cannot be touched with the feeling of our infirmities; (weak, sick, afflicted or to grieve) but was in all points tempted like as we are, yet without sin.
16) Let us therefore come boldly unto the throne of grace, that we may obtain mercy, and find grace to help in our time of need.

We see in this passage that Jesus as our high priest has been touched with the feelings of our infirmities, he has felt weakness, He has been afflicted and He has grieved, He understands our infirmities and He understands what it is to hold a bitter cup. Notice also the hope that is there for us in verse sixteen, *"Let us therefore come boldly unto the throne of grace, that we may obtain mercy and find grace to help in our time of need."*

With this in mind let us look more specifically at Jesus' qualifications as healer of the broken hearted. What are some of the
more specific feelings of infirmities and bitter cup experiences he
has had? We can start with the idea that He left a perfect, sinless
environment to come to earth and dwell among sinful mankind.
Leaving the presence of His heavenly Father so He could come
and die for the sin of the entire world. He knew the emotions of
losing a friend in death as one day He stood at the grave of His
friend Lazarus and wept. He knew the feeling of being betrayed
as one day His friend and co-laborer Judas sold out his friendship
and betrayed Him for thirty pieces of silver. He knew the feeling
of being denied by a friend as one day His friend Peter stood at
a fire and denied that he knew Jesus, or that he had anything to
do with him. Jesus knew the feeling of abandonment as when he
was on the cross all of His disciples accept for John had abandoned
Him. He knew the pain and agony of every sin every person in
the entire world has ever committed because when He was on
the cross all of our sin was placed upon Him. At that point He
also experienced the loneliness of having His Heavenly Father
forsake Him as God could not look upon Jesus Christ while He
was baring our sin. Add to that all the physical pain and agony of
the cross. Before being crucified they took a cat –o- nine tails and
beat Him, the Roman Soldiers hit him with their fists and plucked
out His beard. His body beaten and crucified and at the end of
His crucifixion they pierced His side with a spear at which time
blood and water poured from his side, evidence of a broken heart.
Friend, Jesus Christ, who knows the feeling of a broken heart and
the taste of a very bitter cup is the healer of the broken hearted.

Consider the hands of the healer. I have given this a lot of thought,
I have thought about the hands of an experienced and well trained
surgeon. One who does meticulous work on the human heart!

He is always very careful with his hands. Never putting them in danger of being hurt, it is with his knowledge and training that he knows the healing techniques, but it is with his hands he guides the instruments that can sometimes heal the physical damage to the human heart. With this in mind think of Jesus hands, the healer of the broken hearted. Those hands that were pierced with the nails on the cross of Calvary, Those hands that touched the leper and healed him, no one touched a leper because doing so was a death sentence, but Jesus Christ compassionately touched the leper and healed him in body and in spirit. With His hands Jesus touched the blind man's eyes; he wiped the tears of Mary and Margaret. Those hands that washed the feet of the disciples, the hands that blessed the lads five loaves and two fish which was used to feed a multitude. The hands that wrote in the earth when the woman caught in adultery was brought to Him. Those hands that reached out and calmed the storm and reached out to the Apostle Peter and lifted him up when he began to sink! The hands of Jesus Christ that held the children when they were brought to him! The hands that touched many when He was walking on earth and healed them of their physical, spiritual and emotional infirmities, He is the healer of the broken heart.

He is able to heal you of your broken heart and He is able to give you mercy and grace in your time of need and He will do so as you hold a bitter cup in life. Look to Him and trust Him, the healer of broken hearts!

Chapter 2
ENTERING INTO GETHSEMANE

MATTHEW 6:5-13

5) And when thou prayest, thou shalt not be as the hypocrites are: for they love to pray standing in the synagogues and in the corners of the streets, that they may be seen of men. Verily I say unto you, They have their reward.

6) But thou, when thou prayest, enter into thy closet, and when thou hast shut the door, pray to thy Father which is in secret; and thy father which is in seeth in secret shall reward thee openly.

7) But, when ye pray, use not vain repetitions, as the heathen do: for they think that they shall be heard for their much speaking.

8) Be not ye therefore like unto them: for your Father knoweth what things ye have need of, before ye ask him.

9) After this manner therefore pray ye: Our Father which are in heaven, Hallowed be thy name.

10) Thy kingdom come. Thy will be done in earth, as it is in heaven.

11) Give us this day our daily bread.

12) And forgive us our debts, as we forgive our debtors.

13) And lead us not into temptation, but deliver us from evil: For thine is the kingdom, and the power, and the glory, forever. Amen

MATTHEW 26:36-44

36) Then cometh Jesus with them unto a place called Gethsemane, and saith unto the disciples, Sit ye here, while I go and pray yonder.

37) And he took with him Peter and the two sons of Zebedee, and began to be sorrowful and very heavy.

38) Then saith he unto them, My soul is exceeding sorrowful, even unto death: tarry ye here and watch with me.

39) And he went a little farther, and fell on his face, and prayed saying, **O my Father, if it be possible, let this cup pass from me: nevertheless not as I will, but as thou wilt.**

40) And he cometh unto the disciples, and findeth them asleep, and saith unto Peter, What, could ye not watch with me one hour?

41) Watch and pray that ye enter not into temptation: the spirit indeed is willing, but the flesh is weak.

42) And he went away again the second time, and prayed, saying, O my Father, if this cup may not pass away from me, except I drink it, thy will be done.

43) And he came and found them asleep again: for their eyes were heavy.

44) And he left them, and went away again the third time, saying the same words.

In Matthew chapter six, verses five through fifteen of the Sermon on the Mount, we find Jesus teaching us how to pray and in doing so He instructed us to pray, *"Thy will be done, in earth as it is in heaven."* Thus we are to pray that God's will be done in earth, in our lives, and in the lives of those whom we love.

Then, in Matthew chapter twenty-six, verses thirty-six through forty-four, we find Jesus living the example before His disciples of what He had taught on the mountainside in the Sermon on the Mount. We find Him in the Garden of Gethsemane, at a difficult hour praying, *"Thy will be done."* So we see that Jesus not only told us to pray *"Thy will be done,"* but He also demonstrated how to pray *"Thy will be done"* during the most difficult night of His life and through the most difficult event of His earthly ministry.

Dear friend, in our Christian lives it is not difficult for us to pray, *"Thy will be done"* when we are sitting in the grass at the foot of the mountain on a beautiful day with not a cloud in the sky and all is well with our souls.

It is not difficult for us to pray, *"Thy will be done"* when the only concern in our lives pertaining to the will of God is making a decision about where to go on vacation. Or which restaurant to go to on Friday night, or what color of automobile to buy. But in the darkest hour, when the storm is blowing in with thunder, lightning and blinding rain—praying, *"Thy will be done"* or *"Not my will but thine be done"* takes on a whole new meaning.

Notice in our text Jesus prayed, *"O my Father, if it be possible, let this cup pass from me."* Jesus as the Son of God did not want to be separated from His Father. No son that loves his father wants to be separated from him and Jesus knew that when our sin was placed upon Him on the cross, God the Father would have to look away and at that moment they would be separated.

Jesus, being God incarnate, righteous, sinless and holy, did not want the sin of the whole world to rest upon Him. Imagine for a moment the thought of having the sin of the whole world resting upon you. The sin of every pedophile, rapist, murderer, adulterer, liar, thief; imagine every sin that had ever been or ever would be committed being placed on you. Imagine being put in the position to be sin for the whole world. I would not want that, you would not want that and humanly speaking, Jesus did not want that.

Jesus in His humanity—did not want to suffer physically the pain of the Crucifixion. The Roman soldiers plucking the beard out of His face; taking their fists and hitting Him in the face and placing the crown of thorns upon His head! The terrible pain and anguish of the cat-of-nine-tails being taken across His body thirty-nine times because it was believed that forty times would kill the person being scourged; and then after all of that, being nailed to a cross and hung between Heaven and earth.

Dear friend, humanly speaking, no one would want to suffer that kind of punishment, that kind of physical pain and suffering. But Jesus being the Son of God wanted to please His Father whom He loved. And being the Son of God He wanted to obey His Father.

And Jesus being God incarnate, righteous, sinless and holy wanted man reconciled to God. So in essence Jesus said, "Father your will is a bitter cup—but I submit to your will, I will accept it and I will drink of it."

Sometimes the will of God seems a bitter cup to us. When I was seventeen years old I had a childhood friend that committed suicide; that was a very bitter cup for me. Suicide is never the will of God, the destruction of life is never God's will, but my friend's decision to take his own life left a bitter cup for me to drink. Then approximately one year later another bitter cup was handed to me that I never discuss in detail except to say that it grieved me deeply. It was a situation I could not change; there was nothing I could do about it, I had lost control of the entire situation. I could only take the bitter cup that was handed to me and trust the Lord. Praise God, His grace is sufficient!

Perhaps a bitter cup has been passed into your hands; maybe your husband has left you for another woman and you are rearing your children on your own. Maybe you are a man whose wife has left you for another man.

Perhaps you are a teenager and your mother or dad has abandoned you. Maybe your mother never married your father and you have grown up with out having a relationship with your dad. Or maybe your mother abandoned you.

Perhaps you live in a home with turmoil and heartache. Perhaps your mother or dad is a drunk or on drugs. Maybe you have been molested or abused in some other way. These are all bitter cups. Maybe you deal with physical illness—that is a bitter cup as well. Or maybe you are the caretaker of a loved one who is physically ill.

Perhaps your spouse died prematurely and left you with children to rear and with unfulfilled dreams of growing old together.

Perhaps you have stood in the cemetery to bury a child whom you cherished and for whom you had dreams and ambitions.

Dear friend, I'm saying that sometimes God sees fit to hand us a bitter cup in this life. And when we are handed a bitter cup; what do we do? Where do we turn? How do we accept the cup we are given? My desire is to share with you from the Word of God, what to do when the will of God is a bitter cup.

"God uses broken things: broken soil and broken clouds to produce grain; broken grain to produce bread; broken bread to feed our bodies. He wants our stubbornness broken into humble obedience."
—Vance Havner

Chapter 3

IS IT POSSIBLE FOR THE WILL OF GOD TO BE A BITTER CUP?

JOSEPH'S BITTER CUP

GENESIS 39:1-3

1) And Joseph was brought down to Egypt; and Potiphar, an officer of Pharaoh, captain of the guard, an Egyptian, bought him of the hands of the Ishmaelites, which had brought him down thither.

2) And the Lord was with Joseph, and he was a prosperous man; and he was in the house of his master the Egyptian.

3) And his master saw that the Lord was with him, and that the Lord made all that he did to prosper in his hand.

When we are handed a bitter cup in life, our response is often to ask two questions. One, "Have I done something wrong to displease God that would cause him to punish me?" The second question we ask is; "Is it possible for this bad thing to be the will of God for my life?" Or if I may word the question this way, "Is it possible for the will of God to be a bitter cup?"

To find an answer to this question let us ask some servants of the Lord in the Bible that were given a bitter cup.

We find in our text Joseph the son of Jacob being sold into slavery by the Ishmaelites, who had bought him from his brothers who sold him because they were jealous of Joseph and hated him. The Ishmaelites have placed him on the auction block and Potiphar is going to purchase him like we would an automobile or livestock.

If we could have walked up to Joseph at the moment he stood on the auction block and asked him, "Joseph, are you in the will of God right now? Do you believe that this is the will of God for you to be a slave and to be sold at auction? Joseph, right this moment as you drink from this bitter cup; are you in the will of God?"

Dear friend, I believe that Joseph would answer these questions in the affirmative. I believe that Joseph would answer us with, "Yes, this must be the will of God for my life. I have been handed a bitter cup, and I am going to accept it to the best of my ability and with Gods help I will drink of it!"

We find Joseph in Genesis chapter fifty responding to his brother's concern for the bitter cup that they had a large part in being given to him. In verses 19 through 21 we read, *And Joseph said unto them, Fear not: for am I in the place of God? But as for you, ye thought evil against me; but God meant it unto good, to bring to pass this day, to save much people alive. Now therefore fear ye not: I will nourish you, and your little ones. And he comforted them, and spake kindly unto them."*

Joseph drank of the bitter cup that was given to him and that cup later preserved a nation from starvation, including his own father and brothers and their families.

So Joseph's answer to our question: "Is it possible for the will of God to be a bitter cup?" Is "Yes"!

JOB'S BITTER CUP

When we think of someone receiving a bitter cup we inevitably think of Job and the trials he endured.

JOB 2:7-8

7) So Satan went forth from the presence of the Lord, and smote Job with sore boils from the sole of his foot unto his crown.
8) And he took him a potsherd to scrape himself withal; and he sat down among the ashes.

In Job chapter two we find Job drinking from the bitter cup that he was given. A cup may I add that God allowed to be placed into his hands. We also find Job's three friends coming to visit him.

If we could go to him as he sat down in the ashes scraping him self with the potsherd and ask, "Job, you have lost your children in death, is this the will of God for your life? Job you have lost your wealth, do you believe this is the will of God for your life? Job you have lost your health and your friends think you have committed a terrible sin against God to suffer these hardships, are you in the will of God right now? Job, you are drinking one of the most bitter cups ever given to a man, do you believe that this is God's perfect will for your life?"

Friend, there is no doubt that if we went through what Job went through we would have a lot of questions and most likely a lot of anxiety about what and why God was allowing such things to happen in our lives.

I believe Job best answers these questions when he responded to his friends in chapter thirteen and verse fifteen with these words, *"Though he slay me, yet will I trust in him: but I will maintain mine own ways before him."*

In essence, Job's answer to our question: "Is it possible for the will of God to be a bitter cup?"

Is, yes! It is possible for the will of God to be a bitter cup. And the best thing to do with the bitter cup is to trust the Lord and to do right in His eyes.

Dear friend, I am trying to express two very important thoughts to you in this chapter. One, it is possible for the will of God to be a bitter cup. And secondly, being given a bitter cup puts you in good company. You share a common bond with Job, Joseph, David, Jesus and many others.

Chapter 4
IT'S OK
IF YOU DON'T LIKE
THE BITTER CUP

JOSEPH

GENESIS 40:14-15

Joseph said:

14) But think on me when it shall be well with thee, and shew kindness, I pray thee, unto me, and make mention of me unto Pharaoh, and bring me out of this house:

15) For indeed I was stolen away out of the land of the Hebrews: and here also have I done nothing that they should put me into the dungeon.

I was recently speaking with a young couple who shared with me that they are unable to have children. They have been married for over five years and to their heartbreak no children have been born to them. They have sought medical answers and found that nothing can be done medically to help them. As I spoke with this precious couple who long in their hearts to have a child, the dear Christian lady shared with me that many well meaning people have told her that not being able to have a child is the will of God for their life and they just have to accept that. With tears in her eyes she added, "Dr. Woodard, I may have to accept it, but I don't have to like it!" Her words gripped my heart, after my meeting with them I thought of her words and the sorrow this couple had in their hearts. *"I may have to accept it, but I don't have to like it."* I began to go through the scriptures and study the lives of various people in the Bible who were given a bitter cup, and I began to study their comments and I found that several of the people in Scripture had similar emotions that this young lady had, *"I may have to accept it, but I don't have to like it."* May I say to you right here and now; you may hold a bitter cup in your hands this very moment, and you may be doing every thing in your power to accept it! May I say to you that it is OK if you don't like it?

I believe well meaning people sometimes make a mistake over-emphasizing the words, "This is the will of God, and you just have to accept it!" Perhaps we place guilt on folks and that guilt produces even more depression and sorrow of heart.

It appears in scripture that Joseph had accepted the fact that he had been sold into slavery by his own brothers. He seems to have accepted that he had been falsely accused and put into prison. (*"The dungeon"* is how Joseph referred to the place he was in.) He accepted it, but I do not see any inclination that he liked it.

However, we see later on in the life of Joseph as he tells his brothers, *"But as for you, ye thought evil against me; but God meant it unto good, to bring to pass, as it is this day, to save much people alive."* Joseph spoke these words to the same brothers who hated him, made fun of his dreams and ridiculed him, the same brothers that brought about the bitter cup that Joseph endured. No, Joseph did not like the bitter cup; but he did like the thought of God using him to *"save much people alive."* He did like the truth that God was able to use him through his bitter cup. I'm saying to you that it is OK if you don't like the bitter cup.

JOB

Job 3:1-3
1) After this opened Job his mouth and cursed his day.
2) And Job spake, and said,
3) Let the day perish wherein I was born, and the night in which it was said, there is a man child conceived.

Job said some wonderful things that help us verify that he accepted that his life belonged to God and that God had blessed him in many ways and could do as He pleased in Job's life. I believe that Job accepted his bitter cup to the very best of his ability and made the best of his situation. But I do not see anything that leads me to believe that he liked it. Certainly he did not like losing his wealth and most certainly he did not like losing all of his ten children in death, and I doubt that he liked the boils that covered his entire body. Job cried out to God. He never cursed God. He never was angry toward God. He never quit on God, and even defended God to his wife and to his friends. But he did not like what God allowed in his life, and I am saying to you, It's OK if you don't like the bitter cup.

JESUS CHRIST

Matthew 26:39
And he went a little farther, and fell on his face, and prayed, saying, O my Father, if it be possible, let this cup pass from me: nevertheless not as I will, but as thou wilt.

MATTHEW 26: 42

He went away again the second time, and prayed, saying, O my Father, if this cup may not pass away from me, except I drink it, thy will be done.

MATTHEW 26:44

And he left them, and went away again the third time, saying the same words.

We find Jesus in the Garden praying to the Father with the realization that when He goes to the cross, the sin of the entire world, past present and future, will be placed upon Him; and in that hour for the first time since the foundation of the world He will be separated from God the Father. Being God in flesh and loving all of mankind, Jesus Christ wanted man to be reconciled to God. He wanted to express the love of God to the world, but He did not want to be separated from the Father. Three times Jesus prayed in the Garden, *"If it be possible, let this cup pass from me:"* we read, *"O, Father, if this cup, may not pass away from me, except I drink it, thy will be done."* It is evident that Jesus is accepting the events that are about to take place. He knows that it is the only way mankind can be reconciled to God. He knows that there must be the shedding of innocent blood for the remission of sin and He knows that the hour of anguish ahead of Him is the will of God the Father and that it is the only way to fulfill the salvation of mankind. But it also seems evident that He does not like the bitter cup He accepts as the will of the Father. If He liked it He would not have prayed, *"O my Father, if it be possible, let this cup pass from me."* He did not like the bitter cup, but He did like the truth of you and I being reconciled to God. Jesus Christ did not like the bitter cup of being separated from God the Father while our sin was upon Him, but He sure does love us!

If I could share a personal experience concerning this thought, when my teenage friend committed suicide when I was seventeen years old, I certainly did not like that bitter cup. It devastated me.

However, I do like how God has used the bitter cup of that experience to bring hundreds of teenagers to Christ.

Friend, I do not know what bitter cup you hold in your hands. I do not know what sorrow you may currently have in your life and I do not know what has been the state of your past; but I want to assure you, it is OK if you don't like it. And I believe that whatever God allows in our life. He allows for a purpose. I can not tell you what the purpose of your bitter cup is, but I believe some day He will reveal it to you, if not here, then over on the other side. And until then may our prayer remain, *"Not as I will, but as thou wilt."*

"No journey is complete that does not lead through some dark valleys. We can properly comfort others only wherewith we ourselves have been comforted of God."

—Vance Havner

chapter 5
A LITTLE FARTHER

MATTHEW 26:36
Then cometh Jesus with them unto a place called Gethsemane, and saith unto the disciples, Sit ye here, while I go and pray yonder.

MATTHEW 26:39
And he went a little farther, and fell on his face, and prayed, saying, O my Father, if it be possible, let this cup pass from me: nevertheless not as I will, but as thou wilt.

The night Jesus prayed in the Garden of Gethsemane, He was battling with Satan; this was part of His bitter cup. God allowed Satan to go only so far with Job and just as God the Father allowed Satan to battle with Christ in the Garden, He did not allow Satan to kill Job and He did not allow Satan to kill Jesus Christ. Dear friend, our precious Saviour gave himself willingly on Calvary to die for our sin.

Prayer is our first means of dealing with the bitter cup, going to our Heavenly Father and asking him if it is possible for the bitter cup to pass from us while still accomplishing what He wants to accomplish.

Through prayer we can ask our Heavenly Father if there is some other way to accomplish His will without our having to take of the bitter cup. And if after asking Him if it is possible for the bitter cup to pass from us, He will give us a yes or no answer just as He answered Jesus in the Garden.

Prayer will help you determine the will of God. I am not saying God will give you a full understanding of why you have been handed a bitter cup. I am not saying that God will make clear to you at that moment why you have to deal with the situation you face, but through prayer you will realize that the bitter cup through whatever chain of events and circumstances, is yours to contend with.

If after asking God if the bitter cup can pass from you, you realize that God in His sovereign will has chosen you to receive the bitter cup, prayer will give you the strength to accept it.

Prayer will also give you the wisdom to deal with the bitter cup, without becoming bitter yourself.

You ask is it possible to take from a bitter cup and not become bitter. Yes dear friend it is possible, through prayer. It is prayer that will keep you close to the Lord, it is prayer that will keep your heart and mind focused on the strength of God and it is prayer that will help you go a little farther than you think you can go.

chapter 6
THAT I MAY KNOW HIM

PHILIPPIANS 3:10
That I may know him, and the power of his resurrection, and the fellow-ship of his sufferings, being made conformable unto his death;

The Apostle Paul intrigues me, often referred to as the greatest Christian who ever lived; A man who overcame the sin of his past to accomplish great things through the power of God, for God and to the Glory of God.

In Philippians 3:10 we find an interesting statement made by this great evangelist, *"the fellowship of his sufferings"*. This is especially interesting to me in light of the fact that Paul had caused a lot of suffering through the persecution of believers before his conversion. And now from prison he remarks to the Church at Philippi, *"That I may know him, and the power of his resurrection and the fellowship of his sufferings…"* The Crucifixion of Christ, the most agonizing event in His life, the bitter cup of Calvary, Paul wants to know Him through that? Suffering persecution, beatings, imprisonment, Paul wants to know the Saviour through those things? Well, reality is that none of us want to suffer, we do not want heartache; we do not want a bitter cup. I believe Paul is saying that being faithful through the bitter cup he can know the Saviour better. Often through suffering we are drawn closer to the Lord. As we have mentioned before, a bitter cup can either make one bitter or better. Paul used the things he suffered as a means of drawing closer to his Saviour. Concerning the thorn which Paul had asked the Lord three times to remove, to which God answered Paul, *"My grace is sufficient for thee: for my strength is made perfect in weakness."* (II Corinthians 12:9) Paul responded by accepting the bitter cup of his thorn by saying, *"Most gladly therefore will I rather glory in my infirmities, that the power of Christ may rest upon me. Therefore I take pleasure in infirmities, in reproaches, in necessities, in persecutions, in distresses, for Christ's sake: for when I am weak, then am I strong."* (II Corinthians 12:9b-10) Paul would have rather lived with the thorn, his bitter cup and had the power of God, known the power of his Saviour's resurrection and the fellowship of his Saviour's sufferings than to have had his thorn removed. We must admire the attitude we see in Paul. He accepted his bitter cup, In Philippians 4:11 Paul writes *"I have learned, in whatsoever state I am, therewith to be content."* And he not only accepted it but choose to allow it to bring him closer to his Saviour, the Lord Jesus Christ. This is the same choice you and I have, we can make Paul's statement our prayer, *"That I may know him, and the power of his resurrection, and the fellowship of his sufferings, being made conformable unto his death."* Friend, allow the bitter cup in your life to be a vehicle by which you can know the Lord Jesus Christ in a closer, more, intimate way.

chapter 7
SURRENDER

JOB 1:14-21

14) And there came a messenger unto Job, and said, The oxen were plowing, and the asses were feeding beside them:

15) And the Sabeans fell upon them, and took them away; yea, they have slain the servants with the edge of the sword: and I only am escaped alone to tell thee.

16) While he was yet speaking, there came another, and said, The fire of God is fallen from heaven, and hath burned up the sheep, and the servants, and consumed them: and I only am escaped alone to tell thee.

17) While he was yet speaking, there came another, and said, The Chaldeans made out three bands, and fell upon the camels, and have carried them away, yea, and slain the servants, with the edge of the sword; and I only am escaped to tell thee.

18) While he was yet speaking, there came also another, and said, Thy sons and thy daughters were eating and drinking wine in their eldest brothers house:

19) And, behold, there came a great wind from the wilderness, and smote the four corners of the house, and it fell upon the young men, and they are dead: and I only am escaped alone to tell thee.

*20) Then Job arose, and rent his mantle, and shaved his head, and fell down upon the ground and **worshipped**.*

21) And said, Naked came I out of my mother's womb, and naked shall I return thither: the Lord gave and the Lord hath taken away; **blessed be the name of the Lord.**

We read in this passage of Scripture about Job losing his wealth and his children in death within a brief period of time. We also read Job's response to these tragedies.

Notice, in verse twenty the statement *"and fell to the ground and worshipped."* This was Jobs response to the bitter cup he was given. He worshipped! The word worshipped means to bow self down, crouch, fall down flat, humbly beseech, and make obeisance.

When Job received word of these tragic events, he fell to the ground and worshipped. The truest form of worship is surrender. By bowing himself to the ground humbly, he surrendered to the bitter cup that God allowed Satan to place within his hand. In essence he was saying, Lord if this bitter cup is your will for my life I accept it, I surrender to it. If it is your will that my wealth and my children be taken from me, then I accept your will.

Notice the other statement Job makes in verse twenty-one *"blessed be the name of the Lord."* The word blessed here is describing an act of adoration for the Lord, as to say, lovely is the name of the Lord. Although Job had lost everything at this moment except his health, he was able to say, "The name of the Lord is still lovely".

May I point out here that sometimes—good people receive a bitter cup! It was said of Job that he, *"was perfect and upright, and one that feared God and eschewed evil."* Just because you have been handed a bitter cup does not necessarily mean that you are being punished or that God is angry with you.

If you will recall the event in Scripture of David's son dying that was born to him of Bathsheba. We read in Second Samuel chapter twelve verse sixteen David seeking God on behalf of the child. David prayed and fasted seven days and nights, begging God to let the child live. But God instead handed to David a bitter cup and that bitter cup was the death of his child.

In verses twenty through twenty-three of second Samuel chapter twelve we read David's response to the death of his child. *"Then David arose from the earth, and washed, and anointed himself, and changed his apparel, and came to the house of the Lord, and worshipped: then he came to his own house; and when he required, they set bread before him, and he did eat. Then said his servants unto him, What thing is this that thou hast done? Thou didst fast and weep for the child, while it was alive; but when the child was dead, thou didst rise and eat bread. And he said, While the child was yet alive, I fasted and wept: for I said, who can tell whether God will be gracious to me, that the child may live? But now he is dead, wherefore should I fast? Can I bring him back again? I shall go to him, but he shall not return to me."*

Dear friend, we see in David's response to receiving the bitter cup the word worship, as we saw it in Job's life. David went to the house of God and fell on his face and surrendered to what God had handed him in the bitter cup of his son's death. And after the son's death David accepted the fact that there was nothing more he could do. More prayer and weeping for his son could not bring him back. But surrendering to the will of God could at least bring closure. Knowing that he would some day go to heaven, where his son had gone to be with the Lord, brought hope and comfort in the acceptance of the bitter cup he had been given.

Now let us return to the garden of Gethsemane and the bitter cup of our Saviour. We find Jesus closing his prayer for the third time with these words in Matthew chapter twenty-six verse forty-two, *"thy will be done"*. And in verse forty-four we find Jesus returning to his disciples and saying, *"Sleep on now, and take your rest: behold, the hour is at hand, and the Son of man is betrayed into the hands of sinners."*

There was a point in His prayer that He accepted the bitter cup and I believe He prepared himself to receive it. As He went back to the disciples able to say, *"sleep on now, and take your rest"* in essence Jesus was saying, I have prayed it through; my Father has made it clear to me that this bitter cup is His will for my life and I have surrendered to it. And I have accepted it, I am willing, and now ready to receive the bitter cup, there is no longer a need for you to watch and pray.

I came to give my life for sinners. I have had victory over Satan tonight, and I have surrendered to the will of my Father.

Dear friend, all we can do is accept God's will in our bitter cup when we receive it, and surrender to Him in faith. Surrender to God's will is the beginning of victory and faith in Him is the victory.

BLESSED BE THE NAME OF THE LORD!

chapter 8

GOD CARES THAT YOU HOLD A BITTER CUP IN YOUR HAND

LAMENTATIONS 3:32
But though he cause grief, yet will he have compassion according to the multitude of his mercies.

JOHN 17:24
Father, I will that they also, whom thou hast given me, be with me where I am; that they may behold my glory, which thou hast given me: for thou lovedst me before the foundation of the world.

In John chapter seventeen we find the prayer that Jesus prayed before He went to Gethsemane. It is the real Lord's Prayer and it is a wonderful prayer. In this prayer Jesus is aware of what is ahead of Him. He knows that Calvary is before Him and that He will be given a bitter cup from which He will drink. In His prayer He reminds His father of the love they have. He reminds His father that He knows He has always been loved, even before the foundation of the world.

Dear friend, you can be assured that God the father loves you and that He loved you before the foundation of the world. Jesus spoke of His and God the father's love for you in John 3:16 *"For God so loved the world, that he gave his only begotten Son, that whosoever believeth in him should not perish, but have everlasting life."*

In Romans 5:8 we read *"But God commendeth his love toward us, in that while we were yet sinners, Christ died for us."*

First John 4:10 says, *"Herein is love, not that we loved God, but that he loved us, and sent his Son to be the propitiation for our sins."*

Dear friend, although God may have allowed you to receive a bitter cup, I assure you that He has not forgotten you. He already knows about it, He is aware of all that takes place in your life. He attends the funeral of every sparrow that falls to the ground in death, and He will be with you, with all of his compassion and His multitudes of mercy as you drink of the cup you have received. God loves you more than life; He loves you so much that He gave His only begotten Son the bitterest cup of all to drink from. He cares for you and He is able to see you through the most difficult storm and He will give you strength for the bitterest of cups.

Place your hand in His hand, your faith in His power, your heart in His love and your life into His trust. He loves you! You can sing with assurance that most precious children's hymn, *Jesus Loves Me.*

JESUS LOVES ME

Jesus loves me! This I know,
For the Bible tells me so;
Little ones to Him belong,
They are weak but he is strong.
Jesus loves me! He who died
Heavens gate to open wide;
He will wash away my sin,
Let His little child come in.
Jesus loves me! He will stay
Close beside me all the way;

*"Prayer may not get us what we want,
but it will teach us to want what we need."*
—Vance Havner

chapter 9

DON'T BE CRITICAL OF THOSE WHO ARE UNABLE TO DRINK FROM YOUR CUP

MATTHEW 26:40A-41

"What, could ye not watch with me one hour? Watch and pray that ye enter not into temptation: the spirit indeed is willing, but the flesh is weak."

When we are handed a bitter cup and we realize that other people are not going through what we are going through, that other people appear to have lives that seem to be going well, we tend to be critical of them.

We may even begin to question God with, why do I suffer and struggle with this bitter cup while others do not! Why do I have this situation in my life when other people don't have the kind of problems I have?

This kind of thinking and criticism will make you bitter over the bitter cup. When Jesus came to Peter, James and John and found them sleeping, he did not give up on them and he did not cast them aside. He acknowledged their weaknesses; he stated that their spirit was willing, but that their flesh was weak.

Dear friend, God knows who is able to drink from what cup; he knows who has the strength and who does not have the strength to receive the bitter cup in life. Don't be critical of those who are unable to drink from the cup you have received, but instead strengthen them, encourage them through your faith and trust in Christ to get you through your cup.

A time may come that God's will for their life will be that they receive their own bitter cup, and they being able to look back at how you dealt with yours will give them the strength to accept theirs.

I remind you that although Peter could not stay awake as Jesus prepared himself to receive his bitter cup. History tells us that Peter, after being in prison for nine months was later crucified after being severely scourged. He requested that he be crucified upside down, choosing this a bitter cup for himself, as he felt that he was not worthy to be crucified in the same manner his Saviour was.

I wonder what thoughts he must have had as he made his request to be crucified upside down. Perhaps his mind went back to that night in the garden when the dear Saviour accepted a bitter cup for his salvation while he lay sleeping. Or perhaps Peter recalled how he stood and warmed his hands by the fire denying that he even knew Jesus as the Saviour stood before Pilate taking sips from his bitter cup. Or did Peter look back to that day at the seaside where, after the resurrection, Jesus met with him for the purpose of restoring him to fellowship and re-commissioning him for service?

No doubt Peter remembered the bitter crucifixion of his Saviour and how that Jesus drank from his cup willingly. Perhaps that humbled him to the point that he accepted his bitter cup of execution, upside down. We will never know this side of Heaven what strength and courage we may give to someone else who watched from a distance as we drank from our bitter cup.

Don't be critical of those who are unable to drink from the cup you may be drinking from now, they may have their own bitter cup in the days to come.

Be a blessing to them, not a stumbling block!

Jesus Never Fails

Earthly friends may prove untrue, doubts and fears assail; one still loves and cares for you: one who will not fail.
Though the sky be dark and drear, Feirce and strong the gale, just re-member He is near, And He will not fail.
In life's dark and bitter hour, Love will still prevail; Trust His everlasting power, Jesus will not fail.

— A.A. Luther

chapter 10

DON'T RETALIATE AGAINST THOSE WHO DO NOT UNDERSTAND

MATTHEW 26:47-50

47) And while he yet spake, lo, Judas, one of the twelve, came, and with him a great multitude with swords and staves, from the chief priests and elders of the people.

48) Now he that betrayed him gave them a sign, saying, Whomsoever I shall kiss, that same is he: hold him fast.

49) And forthwith he came to Jesus, and said, Hail master; and kissed him.

50) And Jesus said unto him, Friend, wherefore art thou come? Then came they, and laid hands on Jesus, and took him."

Jesus never retaliated or rejected any part of the bitter cup; he received and accepted all of it. He never retaliated or counter attacked those who attacked him or slandered him. Even in the garden when Judas came to betray Jesus and Peter drew his sword and cut off the ear of the servant of the high priest, Jesus touched the man and healed his ear.

Judas betrayed Christ with an expression of friendship. To kiss someone on the cheek is an eastern custom; it is a method of greeting between friends that is still practiced in the middle-eastern countries. Just as our custom in the United States and several other countries is to shake hands when we greet a friend; Notice also that when Judas greeted Jesus with this custom of a kiss on the cheek, Jesus called Judas friend. *"Friend, wherefore art thou come?"* Jesus knowing that Judas had betrayed him, knowing that Judas had sold his friendship for thirty pieces of silver, yet Jesus never retaliated against him.

It seems that sometimes when we are faced with a bitter cup to bear, those whom we thought to be friends, may betray us, attack us and even condemn us. Just as Job's friends did! Making accusations about his spiritual condition, accusing Job of plowing iniquity and sowing wickedness because of the bitter cup he was given.

The years that I have been in the ministry I have seen good Christian people have to deal with a bitter cup in life. One of those bitter cups in the lives of some has been that of having a son or daughter go astray as the prodigal son who went to the hog pen. It is sad to see these folks condemned and attacked, when that is not what they need. They need true friendship, prayer and encouragement. I have noticed that those who are so quick to condemn are very slow in seeking the restoration of the fallen.

If and when you receive a bitter cup, friends and acquaintances may begin to be critical and try to analyze your situation and make accusations and possibly even betray you. Remember what your Saviour did when betrayed in his bitter cup! He did not retaliate or attack, but he called the one that betrayed him, "friend".

chapter 11
GOD IS IN CONTROL

JOHN 19:8-11

8) When Pilate therefore heard that saying, he was the more afraid;

9) And went again into the judgment hall, and saith unto Jesus, Whence art thou? But Jesus gave him no answer.

10) Then saith Pilate unto him, Speakest thou not unto me? Knowest thou not that I have the power to crucify thee, and have power to release thee?

11) Jesus answered, Thou couldest have no power against me, except it were given thee from above: therefore he that delivered me unto thee hath the greater sin."

Believe and understand this; God has all power! He will not put more on you than you can bear. Or maybe it is more accurate to say that God will not put more on you than he can give you the strength to bear. And dear friend he can give you all the strength you need. God will give you the strength you need to accomplish his will.

Imagine with me what took place in our text in John chapter nineteen. Jesus is standing once again before Pilate in the judgment hall. Pilate is concerned about the response of the people and he is hoping Jesus will give him some way out of his dilemma. In his frustration Pilate announces to Jesus, *"I have power to crucify thee, and power to release thee."*

I can't help but wonder if Jesus didn't laugh under his breath when he replied to Pilate, *"Thou couldest have no power at all against me, except it were given to thee from above."* Did Pilate not realize that he was speaking to the very one that spoke the world into existence? He was speaking to God in flesh, that the accusations that were made about Jesus being God and the Son of God were true.

Did Pilate not realize that Jesus could have had a thought and Pilate would have ceased to exist? The Son of God could have snapped his fingers and twelve legions of angels could have come and carried him away. Jesus could have spoken and had the earth open up and swallow Pilate into Hell.

Dear Friend, it was not Pilate that had the Power that day, it was the one to whom he spoke that had power; Jesus Christ had and has all power. May I remind you that after the resurrection our saviour told his disciples, *"All power is given unto me in heaven and in earth."*?

And if he had all power on the day in which he stood before Pilate, yet drank of his bitter cup, then understand that he has all power still. He has power over your bitter cup. He has the power to give you the strength you need for your bitter cup.

It may seem that the bitter cup you hold in your hands came from Satan. I remind you that Satan would have no power at all except it were given to him from above. Just as God would only allow Satan to go so far with Job, he could take everything, but he could not kill him.

What ever you're bitter cup may be, God has allowed it in his power and in his sovereignty. He had the power to allow you to be handed the bitter cup and he has the power to remove the bitter cup from you. But most importantly, He has the power to help you drink the bitter cup.

chapter 12
TRUST GOD

MATTHEW 26:42FF

...except I drink it, thy will be done.

LUKE 23:46A

And when Jesus had cried with a loud voice, he said, Father, into thy hands I commend my spirit:

As Jesus hung upon the cross between Heaven and earth, with the sin of the world upon him, he prayed once more to God the father. And in this prayer he gave us an example of how to pray in our dark hour of the bitter cup. His prayer was just seven words; *"Into thy hands I commend my spirit."* The word, *commend* which Jesus used in Luke 23:46b means, to deposit as a trust or for protection, to commit the keeping of. There is no better word to describe what took place at that moment as he was dying on the cross.

Jesus Christ the Son placed His spirit into the safe keeping of God the father. He trusted His spirit into the hands of God. This is an example for us to follow.

In our darkest hour, in our drinking of a bitter cup we have some choices to make and one of those choices is to whom we trust our spirit (rational soul, mental disposition), our emotions, our thoughts, our fears, our very being.

We can choose to trust our flesh, we can choose to follow our fears and be overcome by them, we can choose defeat and discouragement, or we can choose to commend our spirit to God the Father; we can choose to trust God.

I also remind you again of Job's words when he took of his bitter cup, *"Though he slay me, yet will I trust in him."* Though you may drink from a bitter cup you can still trust in God, although he has permitted you to be handed a bitter cup, you can place your spirit into his hands for protection and safe keeping.

chapter 13

THE RIGHT WAY TO GIVE UP

MATTHEW 27:50
Jesus, when he had cried again with a loud voice, <u>yielded up the ghost</u>.

MARK 15:37
And Jesus cried with a loud voice, and <u>gave up the ghost</u>.

LUKE 23:46
And when Jesus had cried with a loud voice, he said, Father, into thy hands I commend my spirit: and having said thus, <u>he gave up the ghost</u>.

JOHN 19:30
When Jesus therefore had received the vinegar, he said, It is finished: and he bowed his head, and <u>gave up the ghost</u>.

Jesus yielding up or giving up the ghost is mentioned in all four of the gospels, three times stating it the same way, *"gave up the ghost."* The mission he had come to accomplish was finished and the bitter cup had been consumed.

We saw Him in the garden as he was handed the bitter cup. We saw him before Pilate and throughout the crucifixion as he partook of his bitter cup, and then we see him on the cross at the end, giving up the ghost.

You ask; how does that apply to me? How does what Jesus did in his death help me with the bitter cup I have? May I say that in his death on the cross Jesus not only died for our sin, but he also taught us a valuable lesson about dealing with a bitter cup? Jesus gave up the right way. Dear friend, if you are now drinking from a bitter cup I want you to give up the right way. Don't give up on the Lord, don't give up and quit trying, and don't let discouragement overcome you.

Let me say it this way; Do not give up on God, <u>give up to God</u>. Jesus gave up his ghost, or literally, "dismissed his spirit". This was an act of his will. He died of his own volition. He died to self. Yield yourself to your Heavenly Father. Give up yourself to the Father. Give up your hurt to the Lord. Give up your bitterness to the Lord. Give up your anger to the Lord. Give up your will and do the will of the Lord. When you give up to this extent and die to self, you win!

Dead men do not feel pain, dead men don't suffer, and you cannot do anything to hurt a dead man. I am not speaking of physical death, please do not misunderstand. I am not suggesting suicide. I am talking about when you die of self and give up to the Lord; no one can hurt you.

Jesus surrendered to the will of God before He ever left Heaven for Bethlehem; on the cross He carried out what he had already yielded to. Because of His willingness to surrender to the will of God we have access to His victory. And because He had victory in his bitter cup, we can have victory in ours. But there first must be a giving up to the Will of God.

chapter 14
THE ULTIMATE PURPOSE
OF THE WILL OF GOD

MATTHEW 27:54
Now when the centurion, and they that were with him, watching Jesus, saw the earthquake, and those things that were done, they feared greatly, saying, Truly this was the Son of God.

The centurion solider stated, *"Truly this was the Son of God"*. There could be no other explanation for all that has taken place throughout his crucifixion. He never once tried to defend himself, he did not struggle against the Roman soldiers as they put the spikes in his hands and his feet, but rather gave him self willingly to them.

And then the statements Jesus made from the cross, *"Father forgive them; for they know not what they do."* Luke 23:34) *"My God, my God, why hast thou forsaken me?"* (Matthew 27:46) *"It is finished."* (John 19:30ff) and as he told the repentant thief crucified next to him *"To day shalt thou be with me in paradise."* (Luke 23:43b)

The earthquake, and the rocks rent, and the veil of the temple being rent in twain from the top to the bottom. The dead resurrected. There was no other explanation, there were no other answers except that this one that had denied himself and yielded to the will of his Father, this one, who had laid down his life. This one who had accepted a bitter cup on our behalf, "**Truly this was the Son of God.**"

I cannot tell you what God's purpose is in you surrendering to a bitter cup outside of knowing that it is for His glory. Christ's death on the cross was for God's glory and the glory of Calvary is our salvation.

The bitter cup from which you drink will be for God's glory and at some point will be to help someone else. Your pain will become someone else's strength. Your surrender to the will of God will become someone else's confidence. Your bitter cup will become someone else's perseverance.

Jesus Christ's bitter cup made a way for us to enter into the Holy of Holies!

May those who stand and watch you drink from your bitter cup, with your trust in the Lord Jesus Christ and your surrender to Him, say: Truly this is a child of God!

chapter 15
GOD IS ALWAYS ON TIME

JOHN 11:3-7

3) Therefore his sisters sent unto him, saying, Lord, behold, he whom thou lovest is sick.

4) When Jesus heard that, he said, This sickness is not unto death, but for the glory of God, that the Son of God might be glorified thereby.

5) Now Jesus loved Martha, and her sister, and Lazarus.

6) When he heard therefore that he was sick, he abode two days still in the same place where he was.

7) Then after that saith he to his disciples, Let us go into Judea again.

JOHN 11:17

17) Then when Jesus came, he found that he (Lazarus) had lain in the grave four days already.

JOHN 11:20-21

20) Then Martha, as soon as she heard that Jesus was coming, went and met him: but Mary sat still in the house.

21) Then said Martha unto Jesus, Lord, if thou hadst been here, my brother had not died.

JOHN 11:32

32) Then when Mary was come where Jesus was, and saw him, she fell down at his feet, saying unto him, Lord, if thou hadst been here, my brother had not died.

For Mary and Martha, Lazarus' death was a bitter cup knowing that Jesus could have prevented his death if he would have come to Lazarus when he first heard that Lazarus had fallen ill.

When Jesus arrived four days after Lazarus had died the thought of Jesus waiting two days before coming to Judea made the cup they drank from even more bitter. In their eyes Jesus was late.

JOHN 11:43-44

43) And when he thus had spoken, he cried with a loud voice, Lazarus, come forth.

44) And he that was dead came forth, bound hand and foot with grave clothes: and his face was bound about with a napkin. Jesus saith unto them, Loose him, and let him go."

Jesus stood outside of Lazarus' tomb and called him to come forth out of the grave, arisen from the dead. As it turned out, Jesus was right on schedule! God's time is not our time, we operate on carnal time, we operate on the time of a sin-cursed world, but God operates on eternal time. We see things through carnal, mortal eyes and for the purpose of our own life span, comfort and desires.

All that God does is for His purpose within His eternal time. Mary and Martha thought that Jesus was too late to do anything, but in God's eternal time, Jesus was right on time!

When Stephen was stoned to death, no doubt many of his friends and family members thought that his death was the end of his purpose and that his death was premature. But in Gods eternal time,

Stephen's death was part of His eternal purpose. It was through
Stephen's death that began the conviction of the heart of a man
named Saul of Tarsus, who later became the Apostle Paul and as
we know from scripture, was greatly used of God.

In God's eternal time the bitter cup that Stephen, his family and
friends partook of brought glory to Christ and victory to Paul's
life. When measured in God's eternal time, the experience of your
bitter cup may bring life, hope, courage, blessing, as well as salvation to others.

Only eternity will tell what good you do and what victory you
bring with your bitter cup.

And God Said

I said, "God, I hurt."
And God said, "I know."
I said, "God, I cry a lot."
And God said, "This is why I gave you tears."
I said, "God I am so depressed."
And God said, "That is why I gave you sunshine."
I said, "God, life is so hard."
And God said, "That is why I gave you loved ones."
I said, "God, my loved one died."
And God said, "So did mine."
I said, "God it is such a loss."
And God Said, "I saw mine nailed to a cross."
I said, "God, but your loved one lives."
And God said, "So does yours."
I said, "God, where are they now?"
And God said, "Mine is on my right, and yours is in the light."
I said, "God, it hurts."
And God said, "I know."

chapter 16
GOD CAN GET TO WHERE YOU ARE

MATTHEW 14:22-34

22) And straightway Jesus constrained his disciples to get into a ship, and go before him unto the other side, while he sent the multitudes away.

23) And when he had sent the multitudes away, he went up into a mountain apart to pray: and when the evening was come, he was there alone.

24) But the ship was now in the midst of the sea, tossed with the waves; for the wind was contrary.

25) And in the fourth watch of the night Jesus went unto them, walking on the sea.

26) And when the disciples saw him walking on the sea, they were troubled, saying, It is a spirit; and they cried out for fear.

27) But straightway Jesus spake unto them, saying, Be of good cheer; it is I; be not afraid.

28) And Peter answered him and said, Lord, if it be thou, bid me to come unto thee on the water.

29) And he said, Come. And when Peter was come down out of the ship, he walked on the water, to go to Jesus.

30) But when he saw the wind boisterous, he was afraid; and beginning to sink, he cried, saying, Lord, save me.

31) And immediately Jesus stretched forth his hand, and caught him, and said unto him, O thou of little faith, wherefore didst thou doubt?
32) And when they were come into the ship, the wind ceased.
33) Then they that were in the ship came and worshipped him, saying, Of a truth thou art the Son of God.
34) And when they were gone over, they came into the land of Gennesaret.

Jesus had been ministering to a multitude of people on the hillside. He had fed the five thousand with the lad's five loaves and two fishes and then he instructed the disciples to get into a ship and go before him to the other side. As the disciples were crossing the sea to the other side a storm came and the winds began to toss the ship putting fear in the hearts of the disciples. We are reminded here that sometimes we can be in the will of God and still face storms. The disciples were in the ship Jesus had told them to get into, going where He told them to go and doing what He told them to do, and the ship still came upon a storm. Even when we are in the will of God doing everything that we believe to be right, heartaches can still come into our lives.

As the disciples are being tossed in the waves of the sea we find Jesus walking on the water to the ship and the disciples who are in it. When the disciples saw Jesus they were afraid thinking it was a spirit and the Bible says, *"...they cried out for fear."* Then Jesus spoke to them and said, *"Be of good cheer: it is I; be not afraid."* Now friend, did you ever wonder why it is recorded in scripture that Jesus walked on water. No one else can! I don't know of anyone that has a water-walking ministry, do you? My friend Dr. Tom Williams said that he once asked God why Jesus walked on water and that through prayer God answered to show us that there is no place we can go but that God can still get to where we are. Pause for just a moment and think about that. You may have a bitter cup in your hands, you may have it to your lips, and you may be out in a boat in the middle of the sea with the waves tossing you in the worst storm of your life. You may think that no one can help you; that no one can get to where you are. You may feel afraid and alone. Friend, there is one that can still get to you! He can walk on water! He can come right to your boat. He can walk into the eye of the storm and He can make the wind to cease, He can calm the storm and He can calm you! His words echo with power, *"It is I; be not afraid."*

When the Apostle Peter saw that it was Jesus walking on the water he answered and said, *"Lord, if it be thou, bid me to come unto thee on the water."* Upon Jesus' invitation Peter stepped out of the boat and began to walk toward Jesus; but as Peter saw the wind boisterous he began to sink and in fear he cried out to Jesus, *"Lord, save me."* Notice how Jesus responded to Peter's cry for help in verse thirty-one of our text, *"And immediately, Jesus stretched out his hand and caught him…"* What a joy, what hope we have in the Saviour. Not only can He get to where we are, but He can respond to our cry for help.

Jesus pulled Peter up out of the water and they walked together. Now here is another encouraging truth. After Jesus pulled Peter back up, they walked to the boat and Jesus got in the ship with them. Not only did Jesus get to where they were, not only did He respond to Peter when he cried out for help and pull him up when he was sinking, but Jesus got in the ship with the disciples. May this thought encourage your heart as it does mine! We have a God that can get to where we are in the midst of life's most horrendous storms and He can get in our ship and guide us safely to the other side. For you see, the disciples got to where they were going, they arrived safely at the appointed destination. Jesus told them to get in the ship and go to the other side, and they made it.

Friend, you may have a bitter cup and that cup may be crossing life's sea in a storm. The wind may be blowing and tossing your ship, and you may feel like you are all alone and you may be afraid. But if you will look closely you will find your Saviour has already made it to where you are and He is in your ship. SAIL ON! You will arrive safely on the other shore!

chapter 17
A TIME TO WEEP

ECCLESIASTES 3:1-4

1) To everything there is a season, and a time to every purpose under the heaven:

2) A time to be born, and a time to die; a time to plant, and a time to pluck up that which was planted;

3) A time to kill and a time to heal; a time to breakdown, and a time to build up;

4) A time to weep and a time to laugh; a time to mourn, and a time to dance;

When I was five years old I had my first experience with having someone I was close to die; My Uncle John Freeman. John Freeman was my father's youngest brother and he stayed with us a lot when I was a little boy, he and my grandmother even lived with us for a short time. John Freeman had contracted Polio when he was very young and was crippled in his legs and unable to walk. He would sit on the floor and drag himself around the house, I really don't remember him ever being in a wheelchair. All of my memories are of him on the floor going from room to room or pulling himself up into a chair to sit. In some ways John Freeman was like a child, he never really went to school much. Back in his day physically challenged people did not get to attend school. I have fond memories of John Freeman playing with me on the floor, he would draw me pictures of dogs and horses, and his favorite program was Mister Ed; A comedy about a talking horse. I still have a picture that John Freeman drew for me of Mister Ed and I also have his Bible. My Mother had shared with me that he was very proud of his Bible because he had earned it by being faithful in attending the Ebenezer Baptist church's young men's Bible class.

I remember vividly attending John Freeman's funeral; please do not misinterpret what I am about to say. I have fond memories of attending the funeral. To this day I remember very vividly my father telling me that John Freeman had gone to Heaven; that his body was just a house he lived in while on earth and that when he got to Heaven Jesus gave him a brand new body and he could walk with his new legs.

I remember how happy I was to learn that John Freeman could walk in Heaven. I also vividly remember my Father holding me in his arms at John Freeman's casket and telling me to say goodbye to John Freeman and to tell him that I would see him in Heaven some day. So wrapped in the security of my fathers arms I waved into the casket at John Free-man's old body, (because he had a new one now) and waving I said, "Goodbye, John Freeman, I will see you in Heaven." John Freeman and I were buddies, we were playmates and we were family.

I remember sitting out in our back yard watching the Fourth of July Fireworks just a couple of weeks before he died and to this day I still think of him each fourth of July when I watch the fire works.

Since John Freeman's death when I was a boy it seems that I have seen a lot of people die, both my father and mother are now in Heaven. I have several very close friends who have taken up residence over on that shore that is fairer than day; and of course my close teenage friend who took his own life.

As a former pastor and now evangelist I have assisted in many funer-als and in all of this I have learned some important things about the grieving process. One thing that is obvious to me is that everyone grieves differently. I recall when I pastored, a young couple in my church had baby girl die, she was only three months old, it was heart breaking to see this young mother and father grieve over the death of this precious little child. On the day of the funeral I arrived at the funeral home early to be with the family for their private viewing before all the guests arrived. As we were quietly sitting in the viewing room the mother of the deceased baby walked over and picked the little girl up out of the casket and held her in her arms. The mother sat down on a chair and began to rock the baby, cuddling her, telling her that mommy loves her and weeping. The entire group of people in the viewing room including the funeral director began to weep and a panic fell over many. I quickly whispered a prayer asking the Lord to help me console this young mother. I sat down with the mother and spoke at a whisper. I told her that the baby was very beautiful, that she was a good mother and that her precious little baby was all better now and that little Danielynn was with the Lord. I then began to explain to her that many of her close friends and loved ones were waiting outside and that they would be coming in soon to see her and little Danielynn. I then told her it would be best to put the baby back in the bassinet and tuck her in; I of course was referring to the casket, but I felt that using the word bassinet would be better at that moment. The little mother looked at me with tears rolling off her cheeks and smiled saying, "thank you pastor, will you help me?" I walked over to the casket with her and assisted her in laying little Danielynn's body in the casket and then wrapped a little blanket around her.

Everyone grieves differently. I am reminded in scripture that Thomas was not with the other disciples when word came that Jesus was resurrected, and he did not believe the report. Why was he not with them? Could it be that he was grieving in his own way over the death of Jesus?

A second very important lesson that I have learned about grieving I have learned both from the experiences of others and through my own personal seasons of grief. Allow me to refer again to our text in Ecclesiastes chapter three. Notice in verse one the words, *"To everything there is a season…"* It then goes on to say in verse four, *"A time to weep, and a time to laugh; a time to mourn, and a time to dance."* Now let's consider the meaning of some of the words in our text. The word season here has the meaning of a fitting time, an appointed time or appropriate time. The word, weep means to make lamentation with tears. And the word mourn means to wail, actually to beat the breast and pull at the hair in wailing.

Now here is the thought I want to encourage you with. Whatever your bitter cup may be; the death of a child, the death of a spouse, the death of a parent, a close friend or the death of an uncle who was your buddy when you were five years old, or whether your bitter cup is some other sorrow or heartache; There is a season for grieving; there is an appropriate time, an appointed time to grieve. But there is also a time that we must get back to life and to living. There is a season that we must laugh, and reap and buildup. Whatever or whoever you have lost cannot be replaced, I understand that. But you also cannot afford to lose the blessings that may currently be in your life right now. There are people in your life who are still among the living who need you and whom you need.

I searched the scriptures and found something very helpful and encouraging. It was not what I found in the Bible that helped me as much as what I did not find (even the things we do not find in scripture can sometimes be a blessing). I did not find a believer that grieved for more than forty days. In Genesis Chapter fifty verses one through three we read, *"And Joseph fell on his father's face and wept upon him and kissed him. And Joseph commanded his servants the physicians to embalm his father: and the physicians embalmed Israel. And forty days were fulfilled for him; for so are fulfilled the days of those which are embalmed: and the Egyptians mourned for him three score and ten (seventy) days"*. In the Bible the Egyptians always represent the unbelievers, they did not worship the Lord God; they worshiped many false gods, they did not have the hope that the believers have.

It has been my experience that unbelievers grieve differently than believers. The Apostle Paul wrote to the church at Thessalonica in First Thessalonians chapter four verses thirteen and fourteen: *"But I would not have you to be ignorant, brethren, concerning them which are asleep, that ye sorrow (grieve) not, even as others which have not hope. For if we believe that Jesus died and rose again, even so them also which sleep in Jesus will God bring with him."* The Christian believer has hope; we believe that Jesus Christ is the resurrected Saviour. For the believer death is a temporary departure, and Heaven is an eternal reality. The believer should not be in a continuous state of grieving because we have hope and comfort in the Lord Jesus Christ. For the unbeliever death is a mystery, an unanswered question and seen to most as an eternal goodbye.

In verse ten of Genesis chapter fifty we read, *"And they came to the threshing floor of Atad, which is beyond Jordan and there they mourned with a great and very sore lamentation (expression of sadness): and he made a mourning for his family seven days."* This was a private time of mourning for the family of Jacob. So we see in scripture that the un-believing Egyptians grieved seventy days for Jacob, but his believing family grieved seven days.

In Numbers chapter twenty verse nine the Bible says, *"And when all the congregation saw that Aaron was dead, they mourned for Aaron thirty days, even all the house of Israel."*

Notice in Deuteronomy chapter thirty-four verse eight, *"And the children of Israel wept for Moses in the plains of Moab thirty days: so the days of weeping and mourning for Moses were ended."* Friend there is a season to grieve, it is important to have our private season of grieving, but there is also a season to laugh and a season to dance. As I have shared with you the most grievous death in my life to this point was the suicide of my teenage friend, it was the way that he died that hurt so badly. I have not forgotten him. I still go to his grave, I always remember him on his birthday and every year sometime between his birthday and the anniversary of his death I sit down and listen to a song he liked. It is a song I also chose to have sung at his funeral. I listen to the song and I grieve, I mourn and I weep. I don't want to forget him. I choose to weep, I choose each year to have a season of weeping over the tragic death of my friend. But then I get up, I turn the song off and I get back to life, I laugh, I reap and I build up.

In Second Samuel chapter twelve and verse twenty David realized his baby had died. He had prayed and fasted seven days and nights that the baby might live but it died. Upon realizing the baby had died the Bible says, *"Then David arose from the earth."* Friend he got up! He went and washed himself and changed his clothes and sat down at the table and ate a meal. David got back to living! He had his season of mourning, he then comforted Bathsheba. I am saying it is OK to grieve and it is OK to mourn, but get up and laugh, get up and dance, get up! There is a season to live! The very action of choosing to laugh, the action of choosing to be a blessing to someone else will help you! The action of finding something to rejoice in and then rejoicing in that thing will help you through the grieving process. We must come to a point that we make a conscious decision to enter into the season of healing, building up, laughing, dancing, embracing, and rejoicing. Whatever your bitter cup, consider this order of the grieving process: A time to mourn, a time to heal and a time to laugh.

chapter 18

RESURRECTION MORNING IS COMING

MATTHEW 28:5-7

5) And the angel answered and said unto the women, Fear not ye: for I know that ye seek Jesus, which was crucified.

6) He is not here: for he is risen, as he said. Come, see the place where the Lord lay.

7) And go quickly, and tell his disciples that he is risen from the dead; and, behold, he goeth before you into Galilee; there shall ye see him: lo, I have told you.

Dear friend, you may hold in your hands this very moment a bitter cup, a tragic event that has taken place in your life. Perhaps an illness or the heartbreak of the loss of a loved one; perhaps you have stood at the coffin of a child or a spouse. Perhaps your spouse has abandoned you for another. Perhaps a child has gone the way of the world and rebelled against your love and direction for them.

Maybe you're a young person with the bitter cup of a broken home or with a drunkard father or mother. Or perhaps you have seen the premature death of a parent.

Whatever you're bitter cup may be, you may feel alone, but you are not alone. You may feel that no one cares, But, dear friend there is one that cares deeply for you.

You may feel that no one understands what you are going through with your bitter cup, but I assure you that there is one that understands, for he was handed a very bitter cup and for your sake he accepted it and drank of it.

You may think that you cannot drink it, but you can! You may think that you cannot persevere, but you can! You may think that there is no reason for you to go on, but there is!

For I have good news for you! Resurrection morning is coming! You will rise again!

Jesus, you are going to be betrayed and abandoned by those you love, what are you going to do? Resurrection morning is coming, and I am going to rise again!

Jesus, they are going to beat you and put a crown of thorns on your head, what are you going to do? Resurrection morning is coming, and I am going to rise again!

Jesus, they are going to put you on the cross and the sin of the world will be placed on you, and you will die on that cross, what are you going to do? Resurrection morning is coming, and I am going to rise again!

Jesus, they are going to put you in a tomb and place a stone in the door, what are you going to do? In three days am going to rise again! Resurrection morning is coming!

Jesus, you have a very bitter cup in your hands that your heavenly father has handed you, what are you going to do with it? I am going to accept it and drink it, and in three days I am going to rise again, because resurrection morning is coming!

Dear friend, if you are a born again believer in Jesus Christ, then He who gave Himself for you, He who drank from the bitterest cup of all because He loves you, will not forsake you as you drink from your cup. He that suffered and bled on Calvary for your salvation will give you the strength that you need for your cup. He who stretched out his hands on the cross and in doing so said; I love you this much and then gave His own life that you may have eternal life, is now present with you.

He who overcame death, Hell and the grave, and rose again on Resurrection morning will give you the strength to rise again. Be faithful, surrender to Him and trust Him, drink of the cup now, because your resurrection morning is coming, you will rise again!

When Satan's demons ask; what are you going to do with your bitter cup? Plead the blood of Jesus Christ, then look them in the eye and say, I AM GOING TO ACCEPT IT, I AM GOING TO DRINK IT, AND I AM GOING TO RISE AGAIN, BECAUSE MY RESURRECTION MORNING IS COMING!

Amazing Grace

Amazing grace! How sweet the sound,
that saved a wretch like me!
I once was lost, but now am found,
Was blind, but now I see.

T'was grace that taught my heart to fear,
And grace my fears relieved;
How precious did that grace appear
The hour I first believed!

Through many dangers, toils and snares,
I have already come;
'Tis grace hath brought me safe thus far,
And grace will lead me home.

When we've been there ten thousand years,
Bright shining as the sun,
We've no less days to sing God's praise
Than when we first begun. AMEN!

— John Newton

chapter 19

THESE WORDS ARE TRUE AND FAITHFUL

REVELATION 21:3-7

3) And I heard a great voice out of heaven saying, Behold, the tabernacle of God is with men, and he will dwell with them, and they shall be his people, and God himself shall be their God.

4) And God shall wipe away all tears from their eyes; and there shall be no more death, nor crying, neither shall there be any more pain: for the former things are passed away.

5) And he that sat upon the throne said, Behold, I make all things new. And he said unto me, Write: for these words are true and faithful.

6) And he said unto me, It is done. I am Alpha and Omega, the beginning and the end. I will give unto him that is athirst of the fountain of the water of life freely.

7) He that overcometh shall inherit all things; and I will be his God, and he shall be my son.

Just as there was suffering on Calvary by the Saviour for our sin! And just as sure as Jesus Christ resurrected and walked out of the grave and just as sure as he physically ascended into Heaven! And just as sure as there is going to be a rapture and a resurrection of the dead—there will also be a day when God will settle all accounts. He will reveal to us the answers to all of our questions and He will give us the understanding to all the things that have confounded us on this earth. As the Apostle Paul wrote in First Corinthians chapter thirteen and verse twelve, "*For now we see through a glass darkly; but then face to face: now in part, but then shall I know even as also I am known.*" All the things on this earth that are now unclear to us, on that day He will make clear!

On that day He will follow through with those words that He said are true and faithful, the God of Heaven will wipe away all tears from our eyes. Those tears shed at the grave side of a child shall be wiped away. The tears of the widow and widower, the tears of the orphan, the tears of the lonely, the tears of the brokenhearted and the tears of the wounded spirit! The tears of the caretaker of the terminally ill, the tears of the child whose parent is drug and alcohol addicted. The tears of the parent of a prodigal child, the tears of every soul that ever held a bitter cup in their hands of any kind, along with the tears we have shed over our own sin. God shall wipe away all tears from their eyes.

Then the scripture says, "*there shall be no more death, neither sorrow, nor crying (clamoring), neither shall there be any more pain: for the former things are passed away.*" If I may expound; No more illness, no more heartaches, no more cemetery visits, no more loneliness, no more orphanages, no more setting at the bedside watching a loved one die, no more cancer, no more Alzheimer's, no more wheel chairs, no more chemotherapy. Never again will a child be ill or die.

The gracious God of Heaven will someday take you into His arms and will wipe away all tears from your eyes. Think of it my friend, all the hurt you have experienced, all the grief you have endured, all the pain in this life you have borne, the bitter cup you have drunk from and all the countless tears you have shed—Someday, God will wipe away all tears from <u>your</u> eyes.

chapter 20

WHAT ABOUT THE PALSIED MAN?

Mark 2:1-4

1) And again he entered into Capernaum after some days; and it was noised that he was in the house.

2) And straightway many were gathered together, insomuch that there was no room to receive them, no, not so much as about the door: and he preached the word unto them.

3) And they come unto him bringing one sick of the palsy, which was borne of four.

4) And when they could not come nigh unto him for the press, they uncovered the roof where he was: and when they had broken it up, they let down the bed wherein the sick of the palsy lay.

Upon finishing my first draft of this manuscript I sent a copy to my friend Jonathan Dunbar who lives in Auburn, New York. Jonathan was born with some physical challenges and I wanted his thoughts and advice on this project. Although he has his challenges he also has the heart of a champion. After Jonathan read through the manuscript he called me and we discussed his thoughts. During our conversation he asked me, "What about the palsied man who was carried by the four men to Jesus?" And so I thought, "What about him?" He had a bitter cup with his infirmity! And so after my conversation with Jonathan and following his counsel I want us to consider some things we can learn from the palsied man.

The first thing that comes to my mind is that due to his bitter cup of palsy he was reliant on the assistance of others. He had no other way to get to where Jesus was except someone carry him. Sometimes when we are dealing with a bitter cup we must be reliant on the assistance of others. It is important that we keep a good spirit about these situations. God often places people in our lives that can help us and that want to help us. Do not allow the assistance of others to make you feel sorry for yourself or indebted to them. The truth is if you allow God to work in the situation, those who may be assisting you will often learn from your experience. And the lessons they learn from your testimony, your attitude, your faith and perseverance will be a tremendous blessing to them. Consider the men who carried the palsied man to Jesus. They were probably family members of the palsied man or close friends. They loved him and cared enough for him to take him to Jesus. They had a part in the blessing of what Jesus did to heal him. And consider the idea that maybe the men carrying him did not believe that Jesus could help him but carried him to Jesus because the palsied man believed Jesus could help him. Perhaps he asked them to take him to see Jesus. Imagine how much their faith was strengthened when they saw Jesus heal him.

There is a lesson in the example of the palsied man and his friends for those of us who have a loved one going through the valley of the bitter cup. The men who carried him to Jesus were unable to help him themselves, they could not heal him, they could not change his circumstances, and they were limited in their ability to help him. I am sure they tried to comfort him and make his life better. But there was one thing they found that they could do for him, and it is something we can do for our loved ones who are currently having a bitter cup experience. They took him to Jesus! We can all take people to Jesus. We can take our loved ones to Jesus through prayer. We can pray for those who have difficulties and struggles. For those who are unable to get out we can take Jesus to them by visiting them and reading scripture to them. We can take encouraging books, cards, or recorded music and messages to them that will be a blessing to them. We may sometimes think we are limited to what we can do to help those who suffer. But the truth is there is one very important thing we can all do that will make a difference and sometimes it makes all the difference in the world. We can carry them to Jesus!

So to my friend Jonathan Dunbar from Auburn, New York, thank you for remembering the palsied man and for teaching us through your attitude, testimony and faith in Jesus Christ that there is victory over the bitter cup. Jonathan, you are a true champion!

MY FATHERS WAY

My Father's way may twist and turn,
My heart may throb and ache;
But in my soul I'm glad I know,
He maketh no mistake.

My cherished plans may go astray,
My hopes may fade away;
But still I'll trust my Lord to lead,
For He doth know the way.

Tho' night be dark and it may seem
That day will never break;
I'll pin my faith, my all in Him,
He maketh no mistake.

There's so much now I cannot see,
My eyesight's far too dim;
But come what may, I'll simply trust,
And leave it all to Him.

For by and by the mist will lift
And plain it all He'll make;
Through all the way, tho' dark to me,
He made not one mistake.

— A. M. Overton

chapter 21
HEAVEN

DEAR READER:

This book would be of little help to you if you do not have a personal relationship with Jesus Christ. Accepting his free gift of eternal life is the first step to victory in life and it is the only way to have eternal life in Heaven.

The Bible says,

"For all have sinned and come short of the glory of God." ROMANS 3:23

You and I were born with a sin nature, and we have sinned against God in our deed and thoughts.

"But God commendeth his love toward us, in that while we were yet sinners, Christ died for us." ROMANS 5:8

Although we are sinners God loves us, and he gave his only begotten son, Jesus Christ, to die for our sins in our place. He took our punishment for the sins we have committed.

"For the wages of sin is death; but the gift of God is eternal life through Jesus Christ our Lord." ROMANS 6:23

Because we are sinners, we will die, because death is the penalty of sin. Death is separation; if we die without Jesus Christ as our Saviour, we will be separated from God in Hell for eternity, punished for our sin.

But God's gift to us is eternal life in Heaven with Him forever and ever. In order to receive this free gift of eternal life we must accept it by faith.

"That if thou shalt confess with thy mouth the Lord Jesus, and shalt believe in thine heart that God hath raised him from the dead, thou shalt be saved. For with the heart man believeth unto righteousness; and with the mouth confession is made unto salvation." ROMANS 10:9-10

To confess means to be in agreement. If you are in agreement that you have sinned and believe in your heart that Jesus Christ is the only begotten Son of God, and that He died for your sins, and that God raised Him from the dead. Then you may accept Gods free gift of eternal life.

"For whosoever shall call upon the name of the Lord shall be saved." ROMANS 10:13

If you have never received God's gift of eternal life and would like to do so right now, so that you can have a personal relationship with Him and spend eternity with Him in Heaven, turn from your sin and turn to Jesus Christ. Pray a prayer like this in faith, from your heart.

Dear God, I confess that I am a sinner. I believe that Jesus Christ died for my sin on the cross. Right now I receive through faith your gift in Jesus Christ for eternal life and as my only hope and way to Heaven. Help me to live for you. Thank you for forgiving me and for saving me. Amen!

Dear friend, if you have trusted Jesus Christ as your personal Saviour, please write us that we may rejoice with you. God bless you!

chapter 22
SCRIPTURE READINGS FOR ENCOURAGEMENT

WHEN YOU ARE LONELY

THE PROMISE OF HIS PRESENCE

Fear thou not; for I am with thee: be not dismayed; for I am thy God: I will strengthen thee; yea I will help thee; yea, I will uphold thee with the right hand of my righteousness.

ISAIAH 41:10

When thou passest through the waters, I will be with thee; and through the rivers, they shall not overflow thee: when thou walkest through the fire, thou shalt not be burned; neither shall the flame kindle upon thee.

ISAIAH 43:2

The Lord your God which goeth before you, he shall fight for you, according to all that he did for you in Egypt before your eyes;

DEUTERONOMY 1:30

The eternal God is thy refuge, underneath the everlasting arms: and he shall thrust out the enemy from before thee; and shall say, Destroy them.
DEUTERONOMY 33:27

I am a companion of all them that fear thee, and of them that keep thy precepts.
PSALM 119:63

A man that hath friends must shew himself friendly: and there is a friend that sticketh closer than a brother.
PROVERBS 18:24

For the mountains shall depart, and the hills be removed; but my kindness shall not depart from thee, neither shall the covenant of my peace be removed, saith the Lord that hath mercy on thee.
ISAIAH 54:10

When my father and my mother forsake me, then the Lord will lift me up.
PSALM 27:10

Let your conversation be without covetousness; and be content with such things as ye have: for he hath said, I will never leave thee, nor forsake thee.
HEBREWS 13:5

Sing and rejoice O daughter of Zion: for, lo, I come, and I will dwell in the midst of thee, saith the Lord.
ZECHARIAH 2:10

I will not leave thee comfortless: I will come to you.
JOHN 14:18

PERSEVERE

Looking unto Jesus the author and finisher of our faith; who for the joy that was set before him endured the cross, despising the shame, and is set down at the right hand of the throne of God.

For consider him that endured such contradiction of sinners against himself, lest ye be wearied and faint in your minds.

HEBREWS 12:2-3

Being confident of this very thing, that he which hath begun a good work in you will perform it until the day of Jesus Christ:

PHILIPPIANS 1:6

I can do all things through Christ which strengtheneth me.

PHILIPPIANS 4:13

The Lord is my strength, and he will make my feet like hind's feet, and he will make me to walk upon mine high places. To the chief singer on my stringed instruments.

HABAKKUK 3:19

Nay, in all these things we are more than conquerors through him that loved us.

ROMANS 8:37

We are troubled on every side, yet not distressed; we are perplexed, but not in despair; Persecuted, but not forsaken; cast down, but not destroyed;

II CORINTHIANS 4:8-9

And let us not be weary in well doing: for in due season we shall reap if we faint not.

GALATIANS 6:9

Be of good courage, and he shall strengthen your heart, all ye that hope in the Lord.

PSALM 31:24

He giveth power to the faint; and to them that have no might he increaseth strength.

ISAIAH 40:29

But they that wait upon the Lord shall renew their strength; they shall mount up with wings as eagles; they shall run, and not be weary; and they shall walk, and not faint.

ISAIAH 40:31

But thanks be to God, which giveth us the victory through our Lord Jesus Christ. Therefore, my beloved brethren, be ye stedfast, unmovable, always abounding in the work of the Lord, forasmuch as ye know that your labour is not in vain in the Lord.

I CORINTHIANS 15:57–58

COMFORT IN THE TIME OF GRIEF

But though he cause grief, yet will he have compassion according to the multitude of his mercies.

LAMENTATIONS 3:32

Then David arose from the earth, and washed, and anointed himself, and changed his apparel, and came into the house of God and worshipped: then he came to his own house; and when he required, they set bread before him, and he did eat.

Then said his servants unto him, What thing is this that thou hast done? Thou didst fast and weep for the child, while it was alive; but when the child was dead, thou didst rise and eat bread.

And he said, Who can tell whether God will be gracious to me, that the child may live?
But now he is dead, wherefore shall I fast? Can I bring him back again?
I shall go to him, but he shall not return to me.
II SAMUEL 12:20-23

For the Lord hath comforted his people, and will have mercy upon his afflicted.
ISAIAH 49:13B

Blessed are they that mourn: for they shall be comforted.
MATTHEW 5:4

Blessed be God, even the Father of our Lord Jesus Christ, the Father of mercies, and the God of all comfort.
Who comforteth us in all our tribulation, that we may be able to comfort them which are in any trouble, by the comfort wherewith we ourselves are comforted of God.
II CORINTHIANS 1:3-4

Yea, though I walk through the valley of the shadow of death, I will fear no evil: for thou art with me; thy rod and thy staff they comfort me.
PSALM 23:4

This is my comfort in my affliction: for thy word hath quickened me.
PSALM 119:50

We are confident, I say, and willing rather to be absent from the body, and to be present with the Lord.
II CORINTHIANS 5:8

But I would not have you to be ignorant brethren, concerning them which are asleep, that ye sorrow not, even as others which have no hope.
For if we believe that Jesus died and rose again, even so them also which sleep in Jesus will God bring with him.
I THESSALONIANS 4:13-14

Jesus said unto her, I am the resurrection and the life: he that believeth in me, though he were dead, yet shall he live:
And whosoever liveth and believeth in me shall never die. Believest thou this?
JOHN 11:25-26

And God shall wipe away all tears from their eyes; and there shall be no more death, neither sorrow, nor crying, neither shall there be any more pain: for the former things are passed away.
REVELATION 21:4

WHEN YOU ARE HURT

Let all bitterness, and wrath, and anger, and clamour, and evil speaking, be put away from you, with all malice.
And be ye kind one to another, tenderhearted, forgiving one another, even as God for Christ's sake hath forgiven you.
EPHESIANS 4:31-32

Love worketh no ill to his neighbor: therefore love is the fulfilling of the law.
ROMANS 13:10

Hatred stirreth up strifes: but love covereth all sins.
PROVERBS 10:12

Thou art good, and doest good; teach me thy statutes.

PSALM 119:68

It is good for me that I have been afflicted; that I might learn thy statutes.

PSALM 119:71

To appoint unto them which mourn in Zion, to give unto them beauty for ashes, the oil of joy for mourning, the garment of praise for the spirit of heaviness; that they might be called trees of righteousness, the planting of the Lord, that he might be glorified.

ISAIAH 61:3

Great peace have they which love thy law: and nothing shall offend them.

PSALM 119:165

PEACE IN THE STORM

And he arose, and rebuked the wind, and said unto the sea, Peace, be still. And the wind ceased, and there was a great calm.

MARK 4:39

Let us therefore follow after the things which make for peace, and things wherewith one may edify another.

ROMANS 14:19

Thou wilt keep him in perfect peace, whose mind is stayed on thee: because he trusteth in thee.

ISAIAH 26:3

Be careful for nothing; but in every thing by prayer and supplication with thanksgiving let your requests be made known unto God.
And the peace of God, which passeth all understanding, shall keep your

hearts and minds through Christ Jesus.
PHILIPPIANS 4:6-7

Therefore being justified by faith, we have peace with God through our Lord Jesus Christ:
ROMANS 5:1

WHEN YOU ARE AFRAID

But straightway Jesus spake unto them, saying, Be of Good cheer; it is I; be not afraid.
MATTHEW 14:27

And Jesus came and touched them, and said, Arise, and be not afraid.
MATTHEW 17:7

And as soon as Jesus heard the word that was spoken, he saith unto the ruler of the synagogue, Be not afraid, only believe.
MARK 5:36

Peace I leave with you, my peace I give unto you: not as the world giveth, give I unto you. Let not your heart be troubled, neither let it be afraid.
JOHN 14:27

For God hath not given us the spirit of fear; but of power, and of love, and of a sound mind.
II TIMOTHY 1:7

For ye have not received the spirit of bondage again to fear; but ye have received the Spirit of adoption, whereby we cry, Abba Father.
ROMANS 8:15

He shall cover thee with feathers, and under his wings shalt thou trust: his trust shall be thy shield and buckler.

Thou shalt not be afraid; nor for the arrow that flieth by day;

Nor for the pestilence that walketh in darkness; not for the destruction that wasteth at noonday.

A thousand shall fall at thy side, and ten thousand at thy right hand; but it shall not come night thee.

Psalm 91:4-7

The Lord is my light and my salvation; whom shall I fear? The Lord is my strength of my life; of whom shall I be afraid?

Psalm 27:1

Though an host should encamp against me, my heart shall not fear; though war should rise against me, in this will I be confident.

Psalm 27:3

In God have I put my trust: I will not be afraid what man can do unto me.

Psalm 56:11

So that we may boldly say, the Lord is my helper, and I will not fear what man shall do unto me.

Hebrews 13:6

When Life's Circumstances Are Beyond Your Control

But as for you, ye thought evil against me; but God meant it unto good, to bring to pass, as it is this day, to save much people alive.

Genesis 50:20

And Job arose and rent his mantle, and shaved his head, and fell down upon the ground, and worshipped.

And said, Naked came I out of my mother's womb, and naked shall I return thither: the Lord gave, and the Lord hath taken away; blessed be the name of the Lord.

In all this Job sinned not, nor charged God foolishly.

JOB 1:20-22

What? Shall we receive good at the hand of God, and shall we not receive evil? In all this did not Job sin with his lips.

JOB 2:10B

Though he slay me, yet will I trust in Him: I will maintain mine own ways before Him.

JOB 13:15

For I know that my redeemer liveth, and that he shall stand at the later day upon the earth:

And though after my skin worms destroy this body, yet in my flesh shall I see God:

JOB 19:25-26

But he knoweth the way that I take: when he hath tried me, I shall come forth as gold.

JOB 23:10

Then David arose from the earth, and washed, and anointed himself, and changed his apparel, and came into the house of God and worshipped: then he came to his own house; and when he required, they set bread before him, and he did eat.

Then said his servants unto him, What thing is this that thou hast done? Thou didst fast and weep for the child, while it was alive; but when the child was dead, thou didst rise and eat bread.

And he said, Who can tell whether God will be gracious to me, that the child may live?
But now he is dead, wherefore shall I fast? Can I bring him back again? I shall go to him, but he shall not return to me.
II SAMUEL 12:20-23

He went away again the second time, and prayed, saying, O my Father, if this cup may not pass away from me, except I drink it, thy will be done.
MARK 26:42

For I reckon that the sufferings of this present time are not worthy to be compared with the glory which shall be revealed in us.
ROMANS 8:18

And we know that all things work together for good to them that love God, to them who are the called according to his purpose.
ROMANS 8:28

For I am persuaded, that neither death, nor life, nor angels, nor principalities, nor powers, nor things present, nor things to come,
Nor height, nor depth, nor any other creature, shall be able to separate us from the love of God, which is in Christ Jesus our Lord.
ROMANS 8:38-39

And lest I should be exalted above measure through the abundance of the revelations, there was given to me a thorn in the flesh, the messenger of Satan to buffet me, lest I should be exalted above measure.
For this thing I besought the Lord thrice, that it might depart from me.
And he said unto me, My grace is sufficient for thee: for my strength is

*made perfect in weakness. Most gladly therefore will I rather glory in my
infirmities, that the power of Christ may rest upon me.*

*Therefore I take pleasure in infirmities, in reproaches, in necessities, in persecu-
tions, in distresses for Christ's sake: for when I am weak, then am I strong.*

II CORINTHIANS 12:7-10

*I know both how to be abased, and I know how to abound, every where
and in all things I am instructed to be full and to be hungry, both to abound
and to suffer need.*

I can do all things, through Christ which strengtheneth me.

PHILIPPIANS 4:12-13

Rejoice evermore.

Pray without ceasing.

*In every thing give thanks: for this is the will of God in Christ Jesus
concerning you.*

I THESSALONIANS 5:16-18

"We can not go back and change our past; but we can choose how we allow our past to change us. Our past can either be our master or it can be our school teacher. It can either make us bitter or it can make us better. The choice is ours!"

Dr. Don Woodard
Evangelist

ABOUT THE AUTHOR

Dr. Don Woodard was born in Nashville, Tennessee. His family later moved to Ohio where at the age of five a lady named Georgia Parish knocked on the Woodard family's front door and asked if she could take Donald and Eddie to Sunday school. Through Mrs. Parish's faithfulness the entire family eventually received Christ as Saviour.

In 1993 Dr. Woodard felt led of the Lord to start CandleStick Revival Ministries. This ministry began with a focus of helping churches reach teenagers for the cause of Christ. Today the evangelist travels the country conducting Revival meetings, Teen Crusades and frequently speaks in conferences. Often referred to as "One of America's most loved evangelist to teenagers" Woodard has appeared on television and radio to discuss teen suicide, teen violence, drug and alcohol addiction and family problems in America.

The evangelist and his wife Debbie live on their ranch in Troutville, Virginia. He is the pastor of Beacon Baptist Church in Salem, VA.

DR. DON WOODARD REVIVAL MINISTRIES

LOCAL CHURCH REVIVALS

FUTURE OF AMERICA YOUTH CRUSADES

An evangelistic teen outreach for the entire community through a well-orchestrated plan of reaching into the public schools and reaching teenagers with the gospel.

FLAME FOR REVIVAL CHRISTIAN WORKERS REFRESHER

A three hour course for Sunday school teachers, bus workers, youth ministry and other laborers in the church on working with young people, being an effective Sunday school worker, reaching families through Sunday school and bus ministry and much more.

FRIEND AND FAMILY DAY

A BIG Sunday featuring a special incentive to encourage visitors! Most churches have experienced at least a 15% increase in attendance and some have even doubled their attendance on Friend and Family Day.

YOUTH MINISTRY HELPS

Dr. Woodard has over twenty years experience working with teenagers and developing effective local church teen ministries. He is available for consultation on youth ministry and teen work. And will help your church devise a course of action to develop an effective ministry to teenagers.

CANDLESTICK BAPTIST ORPHANAGE, MAISSADE, HAITI

For Information about Scheduling Dr. Don Woodard for your church or special event please contact him at:

Woodard Revival Ministries
P.O. Box 490, Troutville, VA 24175
540-354-8573
csm2va@netzero.net

ENDORSEMENTS

Don Woodard has written a book that addresses the problems of life and their Biblical solutions. I recommend it highly as a manual on maturity. He has the insights of a time tested man of God.
— Dr. Charles Keen, Minister of Munitions, First Bible International

When The Will of God Is A Bitter Cup is a book of reality my wife and I experienced a few years ago. Our youngest daughter was taken home with Christ in a way that only pointed to God's plan. Dr. Woodard has successfully addressed these kinds of calamities. May you find the peace of God in the aftermath of calamity! We believe this book can help you on that path of reconciliation.
— Pastor and Mrs. Norman (Dorothy) Burdick, Mayville, NY

I was born with Cerebral Palsy and Brother Woodard is a special friend. *When The Will of God Is A Bitter Cup* was a blessing to me. To read of people that God used in spite of their difficulties is an encouragement to anyone with challenges in their life.
— Jonathan Dunbar

Dr. Don Woodard has written a book that will fulfill the purpose for which it was written. If the readers follow the keen and distinctive insights presented they will be strengthened and encouraged in the Lord.
— Dr. Dan Hummel, Beacon of Truth Baptist Ministries

When The Will of God Is A Bitter Cup is a resource of help and strength. We can use this book to be a blessing to our loved ones who possess a bitter cup.
— Dr. Billy Stegall, Pastor